POWER POLITICS
The Reincarnation of Rumpelstiltskin

Arundhati Roy

Arundhati Roy was trained as an architect
and became a screenwriter.
She is the author of *The God of Small Things*
(which won the Booker Prize in 1997),
The End of Imagination (Published by D.C. Books)
and *The Greater Common Good*.
She lives in New Delhi.

A R U N D H A T I   R O Y

POWER POLITICS
The Reincarnation of Rumpelstiltskin

D C BOOKS
2001

POWER POLITICS
The Reincarnation of Rumpelstiltskin
Criticism
by **Arundhati Roy**

Rights Reserved
First Published March 2001
Published by
D C Books
Kottayam-686 001, Kerala, India
Website : www.dcbooks.com
e-mail : dcbooks@sancharnet.in

ISBN 81 - 264 - 0277 - 6

PRINTED IN INDIA
at D C Press (P) Ltd., Kottayam, Kerala, India-686 012

4257 2350 2000
Price Rs. 125.00/US $ 5.99 (HB)
        Rs. 95.00/US $ 3.99 (PB)

CONTENTS

THE REINCARNATION OF RUMPELSTILTSKIN

Remember him? The gnome who could turn straw into gold? Well he's back now, but you wouldn't recognise him. To begin with, he's not an individual gnome anymore. I'm not sure how best to describe him. Let's just say he's metamorphosed into an accretion, a cabal, an assemblage, a malevolent, incorporeal, transnational multi-gnome. Rumpelstiltskin is a notion (gnotion), a piece of deviant, insidious, white logic that will eventually self-annihilate. But for now he's more than okay. He's cock of the walk. King of All That Really Counts (Cash).

He's decimated the competition, killed all the other kings, the other kinds of kings. He's persuaded us that he's all we have left. Our only salvation.

What kind of potentate is Rumpelstiltskin? Powerful, pitiless and armed to the teeth. He's a kind of king the world has never known before. His realm is raw capital, his conquests emerging markets, his prayers profits, his borders limitless, his weapons nuclear. To even *try* and imagine him, to hold the whole of him in your field of vision, is to situate yourself at the very edge of sanity, to offer yourself up for ridicule. King Rumpel reveals only part of himself at a time. He has a bank-account heart. He has television eyes and a newspaper nose in which you see only what he wants you to see and read only what he wants you to read. (See what I mean about the edge of sanity?) There's more: a Surround Sound stereo mouth which amplifies his voice and filters out the sound of the rest of the world so that you can't hear it even when it's shouting (or starving, or dying) and King Rumpel is only whispering, rolling his r's in his North American way.

Listen carefully, this is most of the rest of his story. (It hasn't ended yet, but it will. It must.) It ranges across seas and continents, sometimes majestic and universal, sometimes confining and local. Now and then I'll peg it down with disparate bits of history and geography that could mar the gentle art of storytelling. So please bear with me.

In March this year (2000 AD), the President of the United States (His Excellency the most exalted plenipotentiary of Rumpeldom) visited India. He brought his own bed, the feather pillow he hugs at night and a merry band of businessmen. He was courted and fawned over by the genuflecting representatives of this ancient civilisation with a fervour that can only be described as indecent. Whole cities were superficially spruced up. The poor were herded away, hidden from the presidential gaze. Streets were soaped and scrubbed and festooned with balloons and welcome banners. In Delhi's dirty sky, vindicated nuclear hawks banked and whistled: *Dekho ji dekho! Bill is here because we have the Bomb.* Those Indian citizens with even a modicum of self-respect were so ashamed they stayed in bed for days. Some of us had puzzled furrows on our brows. Since everybody behaved like a craven, happy slave when Master visited, we wondered why we hadn't gone the whole distance. Why hadn't we just crawled under Master's nuclear umbrella in the first place? Then we could spend our pocket money on other things (instead of bombs) and *still* be all safe and slavey. No?

Just before The Visit, the Government of India lifted import restrictions on 1,400 commodities including milk, grain, sugar and cotton (even though this year there was a glut of sugar and cotton in the market, even though 42.5 million tonnes of grain was rotting in government storehouses). During The Visit, contracts worth about US. $ 3 (some say 4) billion were signed.

For reasons of my own, I was particularly interested in a Memorandum of Intent signed between the Ogden Energy Group, a company that specialises in operating garbage incinerators in the US, and the S.Kumars, an Indian textile company that manufactures what it calls 'suiting blends'. Now what might garbage incineration and suiting blends possibly have in common? Suit-incineration? Guess again. Garbage-blends? Nope.

A big hydel dam on the river Narmada in central India. Neither Ogden nor the S.Kumars has ever built or operated a large dam before.

The 400 MW Shri Maheshwar Hydel Project being promoted by the S. Kumars is part of the Narmada Valley Development Project, which boasts of being the most ambitious river valley project in the world. It envisages building 3,200 dams (30 big dams, 135 medium dams and the rest small) that will reconstitute the Narmada and her 41 tributaries into a series of step reservoirs—an immense staircase of enslaved water. It will alter the ecology of an entire river basin, affect the lives of 25 million people who live in the valley, submerge 4,000 sq km of old growth, deciduous forest, hundreds of temples, as well as archaeological sites dating back to the lower Palaeolithic age.

The dams that have been built on the river so far are all government projects. The Maheshwar Dam is slated to be India's first major *private* hydel power project.

What is interesting about it is not only that it's part of the most bitterly opposed river valley project in India, but also that it is a strand in the skein of a mammoth global enterprise. Understanding what is happening in Maheshwar, decoding the nature of the deals that are being struck between two of the world's great democracies, will go a long way towards gaining a rudimentary grasp of what is being done to us, while we, poor fools, stand by and clap and cheer and hasten things along. (When I say 'us' I mean *people*, human beings. Not countries, not governments.)

Personally, I took the first step towards arriving at this understanding when, over a few days in March this year (2000 AD), I lived through a writer's bad dream. I witnessed the ritualistic slaughter of Language as I know and understand it. Let me explain.

On the very days that President Clinton was in India, in far away Holland, the World Water Forum was convened. Three thousand and five hundred bankers, businessmen, government ministers, policy writers, engineers, economists (and, in order to pretend that the 'other side' was also represented—a handful of activists, indigenous dance troupes, impoverished street theatre groups and half a dozen young girls dressed as inflatable silver faucets) gathered at The Hague to discuss the future of the world's water. Every speech was generously peppered with phrases like 'women's empowerment', 'people's participation' and 'deepening democracy'. Yet it turned out that the whole purpose of the Forum was to press for the privatisation of the world's water. There was pious talk of having access to drinking water declared a Basic Human Right. How would this be implemented, you might ask. Simple. By putting a *market value* on water. By selling it at its 'true' price. (It's common knowledge that water is becoming a scarce resource. One billion people in the world have no access to drinking water.) The 'market' decrees that the scarcer something is, the more expensive it becomes. So the talk of connecting human rights to a 'true price' was more than a little baffling. At first I didn't quite get their drift—did they believe in human rights for the rich, or that only the rich are human or that all humans are rich? But I see it now. A shiny, climate-controlled human rights supermarket with a clearance sale on Christmas day.(A small but necessary clarification: there is a difference between *valuing* water and putting a *market value* on water . No one values water more than a village woman who has to walk miles to fetch it. No one values it less than urban folk who pay for it to flow endlessly at the turn of a tap.)

One marrowy American panelist put it rather nicely—"God gave us the rivers," he drawled, "but he did't put in the delivery systems. That's why we need private enterprise." No doubt with a little Structural Adjustment to the rest of the things God gave us, we could all live in a simpler world *(If all the seas were one sea, what a big sea it would be...)*—Evian could own the water, Rand the earth, Enron the air. Old Rumpelstiltskin could be the handsomely paid supreme CEO.

When all the rivers and valleys and forests and hills of the world have been priced, packaged, barcoded and stacked in the local supermarket, when all the hay and coal and earth and wood and water has been turned to gold, what then shall we do with all the gold? Make nuclear bombs to obliterate what's left of the ravaged landscapes and the notional nations in our ruined world?

As a writer one spends a lifetime journeying into the heart of language, trying to minimise, if not eliminate, the distance between language and thought. 'Language is the skin on my thought', I remember saying to someone who once asked what language meant to me. At The Hague I stumbled on a denomination, a sub-world, whose life's endeavour was entirely the opposite of mine. For them the whole purpose of language was to *mask* intent. They earn their abundant livings by converting bar graphs that plot their companies' profits into consummately written, politically exemplary, socially just policy documents that are impossible to implement and designed to remain forever on paper, secret even (especially) from the people they're written for. They breed and prosper in the space that lies between what they say and what they sell. What they're lobbying for is not simply the privatisation of natural resources and essential infrastructure, but the privatisation of policy making itself. Dam-builders want to control public water policies. Power utility companies want to draft power policies and financial institutions want to supervise government disinvestment.

Let's begin at the beginning. What does privatisation *really* mean? Essentially, it is the transfer of public productive assets from the State to private companies. Productive assets include natural resources. Earth, forest, water, air. These are assets that the State holds in trust for the people it represents. In a country like India, 70 per cent of the population lives in rural areas. That's 700 million people. Their lives depend directly on access to natural resources. To snatch these away and sell them as stock to private companies is a process of barbaric dispossession on a scale that has no parallel in history. What happens when you 'privatise' something as essential to human survival as water? What happens when you commodify water and say that only those who can come up with the cash to pay the 'market price' can have it? In 1999, the government of Bolivia privatised the public water supply system in the city of Cochacomba, and signed a 40-year lease with Bechtel, a giant US engineering firm. The first thing Bechtel did was to triple the price of water. Hundreds of thousands of people simply couldn't afford it any more. Citizens came out on the streets to protest. A transport strike brought the entire city to a standstill. Hugo Banzer, the former Bolivian dictator (now the President) ordered the police to fire at the crowds. Six people were killed, 175 injured and two children blinded. The protest continued because people had no options—what is the option to thirst? In April 2000, Banzer declared Martial Law. The protest continued. Eventually Bechtel was forced to flee its offices. Now it's trying to extort a $ 12 million exit payment from the Bolivian government.

Cochacomba has a population of half a million people. Think of what would happen in an Indian city. Even a small one.

Rumpelstiltskin thinks big. Today he's stalking mega-game: dams, mines, armaments, power plants, public water supply systems, telecommunication systems, the management and dissemination of knowledge, biodiversity, seeds (he wants to own life and the very process of reproduction) and the industrial infrastructure that supports all this. His minions arrive in Third World countries masquerading as missionaries come to redeem the wretched. They have a completely different dossier in their briefcases. To understand what they're *really* saying (selling), you have to teach yourself to unscramble their vernacular.

Recently, John Welch, chairman of General Electric (GE), was on TV in India. "I beg and pray to the Indian Government to improve infrastructure," he said, and added touchingly, "Don't do it for GE's sake, do it for yourselves." He went on to say that privatising the power sector was the only way to bring India's one billion people into the digital network. "You can talk about information and intellectual capital, but without the power to drive it, you will miss the next revolution."

What he meant, of course, was: "You are a market of one billion customers. If you don't buy our equipment, *we* will miss the next revolution."

Will someone please tell him that of his one billion 'customers', 400 million are illiterate and live without even one square meal a day, and 200 million have no access to safe drinking water? Being brought into the 'digital framework' is hardly what's uppermost on their minds.

The story behind the story is as follows: there are six corporations that dominate the production of power generation equipment in the world. GE is one of them. Together, each year they manufacture (and therefore need to sell) equipment that can generate 20,000 MW of power. For a variety of reasons there is little (read almost zero) additional demand for power equipment in the First World. This leaves these mammoth multinationals with a redundant capacity that they desperately need to offload. India and China are their big target markets, because between these two countries, the demand for power-generating equipment is 10,000 MW per year.

The First World needs to sell, the Third World needs to buy—it ought to be a reasonable business proposition. But it isn't. For many years, India has been more or less self sufficient in power equipment. The Indian public sector company, Bharat Heavy Electricals Ltd. (BHEL), manufactured and even exported world-class power equipment. All that's changed now. Over the years, our own government has starved it of orders, cut off funds for research and development and more or less edged it out of a dignified existence. Today BHEL is no more than a sweat shop. It is being forced into 'joint ventures' (one with GE and one with Siemens) where its only role is to provide cheap, unskilled labour while they provide the equipment and the technology. Why? Why does more expensive, imported foreign equipment suit our bureaucrats and politicians better? We all know why. Because graft is factored into the deal. Buying equipment from your local store is just not the same thing. It's not surprising that almost half the officials named in the Jain Hawala scandal were officials from the power sector involved with the selection and purchase of power equipment.

The privatisation of power (felicitous phrase!) is at the top of the Indian government's agenda. The US is the single largest foreign investor in the power sector (which, to some extent, explains The Visit). The argument being advanced (both by the government and by the private sector) in favour of privatisation is that over the last 50 years the government has bungled its brief. It has failed to deliver. The State Electricity Boards (SEBs) are insolvent. Inefficiency, corruption, theft, and heavy subsidies have run them into the ground.

In the push for privatisation, the customary depiction of the corrupt, oily, Third World government official, selling his country's interests for personal profit, fits perfectly into the scheme of things. The private sector bristles accusingly. The government coyly acknowledges the accusation and pleads its inability to reform itself. In fact it goes out of its way to exaggerate its own inefficiencies. This is meant to come across as refreshing candour. In a speech he made just before he died, P.R. Kumaramangalam, minister for power, said that the overall figure of loss and deficit in the power sector was Rs. 37,000 crore. He went on to say that India's transmission and distribution (T&D) losses are between 35 and 40 per cent. Of the remaining 60 per cent, according to the minister, billing is restricted to only 40 per cent. His conclusion: that only about quarter of the electricity that is produced in India is metered. Official sources say that this is a somewhat exaggerated account. The situation is bad enough, it doesn't need to be exaggerated. According to figures put out by the power ministry, the national average T&D losses are 23 per cent. (In 1947 it was 14.39 per cent). Even without the minister's hyperbole, this puts India in the same league as countries with the *worst* T&D losses in the world, like the Dominican Republic, Myanmar and Bangladesh.

The solution to this malaise, we discover, is not to improve our housekeeping skills, not to try and minimise our losses, not to force the state to be more accountable, but to permit it to abdicate its responsibility altogether and privatise the power sector. Then magic will happen. Economic viability and Swiss-style efficiency will kick in like clockwork.

But there's a sub-plot missing in this narrative. Over the years, the SEBs have been bankrupted by massive power thefts. Who's stealing the power? Some of it no doubt is stolen by the poor-slum dwellers, people who live in unauthorised colonies on the fringes of big cities. But they don't have the electrical gadgetry to consume the quantum of electricity we're talking about. The big stuff, the megawatt thievery, is orchestrated by the industrial sector in connivance with politicians and government officers.

Consider as an example the state of Madhya Pradesh in which the Maheshwar Dam is being built. Seven years ago it was a power surplus state. Today it finds itself in an intriguing situation. Industrial demand has *declined* by 30 per cent. Power production has *increased* from 3,813 MW to 4,025 M.W. And the

State Electricity Board is showing a loss of Rs 1,200 crore. An inspection drive solved the puzzle. *It found that 70 per cent of the industrialists in the state steal Electricity!* The theft adds up to a loss of nearly Rs 500 Crore. That's 41 per cent of the total deficit. Madhya Pradesh is by no means an unusual example. States like Orissa, Andhra Pradesh, and Delhi have T&D losses of between 30 & 50 per cent (Way over the national average) which indicate massive power theft.

No one talks very much about this. It's so much nicer to blame the poor. The average economist, planner or drawing room intellectual will tell you that the SEBs have gone belly up for two reasons: (a) Because 'political compulsions' ensure that domestic power tariffs are kept unviably low, and (b) Because subsidies given to the farm sector result in enormous hidden losses.

The first step that a 'reformed' privatised power sector is expected to take is to cut agricultural subsidies and put a 'realistic' tariff (market value) on power.

What are political compulsions? Why are they considered such a bad thing? Basically, it seems to me, 'political compulsions' is a phrase that describes the fancy footwork that governments have to perform in order to strike a balance between redeeming a sinking economy and serving an impoverished electorate. Striking a balance between what the 'market' demands and what people can afford, is—or certainly ought to be—the primary, fundamental responsibility of any democratic government. Privatisation seeks to disengage politics from the 'market'. To do that would be to blunt the very last weapon that India's poor still have—their vote. Once that's gone, elections will become (even more of) a charade than they already are and democracy will just become the name of a new rock band. The poor will be absent from the negotiating table. They will simply cease to matter.

But the cry has already gone up. The demand to cut subsidies has almost become a blood sport. It's a small world. Bolivia's only a short walk down the road from here.

When it recommends 'privatising the power sector', does the government mean that it is going to permit just anybody who wishes to generate power to come in and compete in a free market? Of course not. There's nothing free about the market in the power sector. Reforming the power sector in India means that the concerned state government underwrites preposterously one-sided power purchase Agreements with select companies, preferably huge multinationals. Essentially, it is the transfer of assets and infrastructure from bribe-taker to bribe-giver, which involves more bribery than ever. Once the agreements are signed, they are free to produce power at exorbitant rates that no one can afford. Not even, ironically enough, the Indian industrialists who have been rooting for them all along. They, poor chaps, end up like vultures on a carcass that get chased off by a visiting hyena.

Nothing illustrates this process better than the story of Enron of the US, the first private power project in India. The first Power Purchase Agreement between Enron and the Congress-ruled state government of Maharashtra for a 695 MW power plant was signed in 1993. The opposition parties, the BJP and the Shiv Sena, set up a howl of 'Swadeshi' protest, and filed legal proceedings against Enron and the state government. They alleged malfeasance and corruption at the highest level. A year later, when state elections were announced, it was the *only* compaign issue of the BJP-Shiv Sena alliance.

In February 1995, this combine won the elections. True to their word, they "scrapped" the project. In a savage, fiery statement, Mr Advani attacked the phenomenon of what he called "loot-through-liberalisation". He more or less directly accused the Congress government of having taken a Rs 62-crore bribe from Enron. Following the annulling of the contract, the US government began to pressurise the Maharashtra government. US Ambassador Frank Wisner made several statements deploring the cancellation. (The day he completed his term as Ambassador, he joined Enron as a director). In November 1995, the BJP-Shiv Sena government of Maharashtra announced a 'renegotiation' committee. In may 1996, a minority government headed by the BJP was sworn in at the Centre. It lasted for exactly 13 days and then resigned before facing a vote of no-confidence in the Lok Sabha. On its last day in office, even as the no-confidence motion was in progress, the Cabinet met for a hurried 'lunch' and re-ratified the Central Government's counter-guarantee (that had become void because of the earlier 'cancelled' contract with Enron). In August 1996, the government of Maharashtra signed a fresh contract with Enron on terms that would astound the most hardboiled cynic.

The impugned contract had involved annual payments to Enron of US $ 430 million for phase I (695 MW) of the project, with phase II (2,015 MW) being optional. The 're-negotiated' Power Purchase Agreement makes phase II of the project *mandatory* and legally binds the Maharashtra State Electricity Board (MSEB) to pay Enron a some of US $ 30 *billion*!

It constitutes the largest contract ever signed in the history of India. In effect for an increase in installed capacity of 18 per cent, the MSEB has to set aside 70 per cent of its revenue to be able to pay Enron. There is, of course, no record of what mathematical formula was used to compute the ' re-negotiated' bribe. Nor any trace of how much trickled up or down or sideways and to whom.

But there's more: in one of the most extraordinary decisions in its not entirely pristine history, in April 1997, the Supreme Court of India refused to entertain an appeal against Enron.

Today, four years later, everything that critics of the project predicted has come true with an eerie vengeance. The power that the Enron plant produces is *twice* as expensive as its nearest competitor and *seven times* as expensive as the cheapest electricity available in Maharashtra. In May 2000, the Maharashtra Electricity Regulatory Committee (MERC) ruled that temporarily until as long as was absolutely necessary, *no* power should be brought from Enron. It was based on a calculation that it would be cheaper to just pay Enron the mandatory fixed charges for the maintenance and administration of the plant that they are contractually obliged to pay than to actually buy any of its exorbitant power. The fixed charges alone work out to Rs 1,000 crore a year for phase I of the project. Phase II will be nearly twice the size.

A thousand crore a year for the next 40 years.

Meanwhile, industrialists in Maharashtra have begun to generate their own power at a much cheaper rate, with private generators. The demand for power from the industrial sector has begun to decline rapidly. The State Electricity Board, strapped for cash, with Enron hanging like an albatross around its neck, will now have no choice but to make private gensets illegal. That's the only way that industrialists can be coerced into buying Enron's exorbitant electricity.

Now, what was that again, Mr Advani? *Looting through liberalisation ?* What a fine, upstanding leader you are.

Here's to the Hindutva brand of Swadeshi. Here's to the 'free' market. Here's to forked tongues.

Having said all this, there's no doubt that there *is* a power-shortage crisis in India. But there's another, more serious crisis on hand.

Planners in India boast that India consumes 20 times more electricity today than it did 50 years ago. They use it as an index of progress. They omit to mention that 70 per cent of rural households still have no electricity. In the poorest states, Bihar, Uttar Pradesh, Orissa and Rajasthan, over 85 per cent of the poorest people, mostly Dalit and Adivasi households, have no electricity. What a shameful, shocking record for the world's biggest democracy.

Unless this crisis is acknowledged and honestly addressed, generating "lots and lots of power" (as Mr Welch put it) will only mean that it will be siphoned off by the rich with their endless appetites. It will require a very imaginative, very radical form of 'structural adjustment' to right this.

'Privatisation' is presented as being the only alternative to an inefficient, corrupt State. In fact, it's not a choice at all. It's only made to *look* like one. Essentially, privatisation is a mutually profitable business contract between the private (preferably foreign) company/ financial institution, and the ruling elite of the Third World. (One of the fallouts is that it makes corruption an elitist affair. Your average small-fry government official is in grave danger of losing his or her bit on the side.)

India's politicians have virtually mortgaged their country to the World Bank. Today India pays back more money in interest and repayment instalments than it receives. It is forced to incur new debts in order to repay old ones. In other words, it's exporting capital. Of late, however, institutions like the World Bank and the IMF that have bled the Third World all these years, look like benevolent saints compared to the new mutants in the market. These are known as ECAs—Export Credit Agencies. If the World Bank is a colonising army hamstrung by red tape and bureaucracy, the ECAs are freewheeling, marauding mercenaries. Basically, ECAs insure private companies operating in foreign countries against commercial and political risks. The device is called an export credit guarantee. It's quite simple, really. No First World private company wants to export capital or goods or services to a politically and /or economically unstable country without insuring itself against unforeseen contingencies. So the private company covers itself with an export credit guarantee. The ECA, in turn, has an agreement with the government of its own country. The government of its own country has an agreement with the government of the importing country. The upshot of this fine imbrication is that if a situation does arise in which the ECA has to pay its client, its own government pays the ECA and recovers its money by adding it to the bilateral debt owed by the importing country. (So the real guarantors are actually, once again, the Third World poor). Complicated, but cool. And foolproof.

The quadrangular private company-ECA-government-government formation neatly circumvents political accountability. Though they're all actually business associates, flak from noisy, tiresome NGOs and activist groups can be diverted and funnelled to the ECA, where, like noxious industrial effluent, it lies in cooling ponds before being disposed of. The attraction of the ECAs (for both governments and private companies) is that they are secretive and don't bother with tedious details like human rights violations and environmental guidelines. (The rare ones that do, like the US Exim Bank, are under pressure to change). It short-circuits lumbering World Bank-style bureaucracy. It makes projects like Big Dams (which involve the displacement and impoverishment of large numbers of people, which in turn is politically risky) that much easier to finance. With an ECA guarantee, 'developers' can go ahead and dig and quarry and mine and dam the hell out of peoples' lives without having to even address, never mind answer, embarrassing questions.

Now, coming back to Maheshwar...

In order to place India's first private Big Dam in perspective, I need to briefly set out the short, vulgar history of Big Dams in India in general and on the Narmada in particular.

The international dam industry alone is worth US $ 20 billion a year. In the First World, dams are being decommissioned, blown up. That leaves us with another industry threatened with redundancy desperately in search of dumping grounds. Fortunately (for the industry), most Third World countries, India especially, are deeply committed to Big Dams.

India has the third-largest number of Big Dams in the world. Three thousand and six hundred Indian dams qualify as Big Dams under the ICOLD (International Committee on Large Dams) definition. Six hundred and ninety-five more are under construction. This means that 40 per cent of all the Big Dams being built in the world are being built in India. For reasons more cynical than honourable, politicians and planners have successfully portrayed Big Dams to an unquestioning public as symbols of nationalism— huge, wet, cement flags. Nehru's speech about Big Dams being "the temples of modern India" has made its way into primary school text-books in every Indian language. Every school child is taught that Big Dams will deliver the people of India from hunger and poverty.

Will they? Have they?

To merely *ask* these questions is to invite accusations of sedition, of being anti-national, of being a spy, and, most ludicrous of all—of receiving 'foreign funds'. The distinguished Mr Advani (home minister now), while speaking at the inauguration of construction at the Sardar Sarovar Dam site on 31st of October, said that the three greatest achievements of his government were: the nuclear tests in 1998, the Kargil war in 1999, and the Supreme Court verdict in favour of the construction of the Sardar Sarovar Dam in 2000. He called it a victory for "development nationalism" (a twisted variation of cultural nationalism). For the home minister to call a Supreme Court verdict a victory for his government doesn't say much for the Supreme Court. I have no quarrel with his clubbing together nuclear bombs, big dams and wars. However, calling them 'achievements' is sinister. Mr Advani then went on to make farcical allegations about how those of us who were against the dam were the 'same people' who protested against the nuclear tests and implied that we were in league with 'foreign agencies who don't want India to develop'. Unfortunately, this is not imbecilic paranoia. It's a deliberate, dangerous attempt to suppress outrageous facts by whipping up mindless mob frenzy. He did it in the run up to the destruction of the Babri Masjid. He's doing it again. He has given notice that he will stop at nothing. Those who come in his way will be dealt with by any methods he deems necessary.

Nevertheless, there is too much at stake to remain silent. After all, we don't want to be like good middle-class Germans in the '30s, who drove their children to piano classes and never noticed the concentration camps springing up around them—or do we? There are questions that must be asked. And answered. There is space here for no more than a brief summary of the costs and benefits of Big Dams. A brief summary is all we need.

Ninety per cent of the Big Dams in India are irrigation dams. They are the key, according to planners, of India's 'food security'.

So how much food do Big Dams produce?

The extraordinary thing is that there is no official government figure for this.

The India Country Study section in the World Commission on Dams Report, (released in London on the 16th of November by Nelson Mandela) was prepared by a team of experts—the former secretary of water resources, the former director of the Madras Institute of Development Studies, a former secretary of the Central Water Commission and two members of the faculty of the Indian Institute of Public Administration.

One of the chapters in the study deduces that the contribution of large dams to India's foodgrain produce is less than 10 per cent. *Less Than Ten Percent!*

Ten per cent of the total produce currently

works out to 20 million tonnes. This year, more than double that amount (42.5 million tonnes) is rotting in government storehouses while at the same time 350 million Indian citizens live below the poverty line *(and while grain is actually being imported!)*. The Ministry of food and civil supplies says that 10 percent of India's total foodgrain produce is eaten every year by rats. India must be the only country in the world that builds dams, uproots millions of people, submerges thousands of hectares of forest, in order to feed rats.

It's hard to believe that things can go so grievously, so perilously wrong. But they have. It's understandable that those who are responsible find it hard to own up to their mistakes, because Big Dams did not start out as a cynical enterprise. They began as a dream. They have ended as grisly nightmare. It's time to wake up.

So much for the benefits of India's Big Dams. Let's take a look at the costs. How many people have been displaced by Big Dams?

Once again, there is no official record.

In fact there's no record at all. This is unpardonable on the part of the Indian State. And unpardonable on the part of planners, economists, funding agencies and the rest of the urban intellectual community who are so quick to rise up in defence of Big Dams.

Last year, just in order to do a sanity check, I extrapolated an average from a study of 54 dams done by the Indian Institute of Public Administration. After *quartering* the average they arrived at, my very conservative estimate of the number of people displaced by Big Dams in India over the last 50 years was 33 million people.

This was jeered at by some economists and planners as being a preposterously exaggerated figure.

India's secretary for Rural Development put the figure at 40 million.

Today, a chapter in the India Country Study says the figure could be as high as 56 million people.

That's twice the population of Canada. More than three times the population of Australia.

Think about it: 56 million people displaced by Big Dams in the last 50 years. And India *still* does not have a national rehabilitation policy.

When the history of India's miraculous leap to the forefront of the Information Revolution is written, let it be said that 56 million Indians (and their children's children) paid for it with everything they ever had. Their homes, their lands, their languages, their histories.

You can see them from your car window when you drive home every night. Try not to look away. Try to meet their eyes. Fifty-six million displaced, impoverished, pulverised people. Over 60 per cent of them are Dalit and Adivasi. (There is devastating meaning couched in this figure.) There's a saying in the villages of Narmada Valley—"You can wake someone who's sleeping. But you can't wake someone who's *pretending* to be asleep". When it comes to the politics of forced, involuntary displacement, there's a deafening silence in this country. People's eyes glaze over. They behave as though it's just a blip in the democratic process. The nicer ones say, 'Oh, but it's such a pity. People *must* be resettled' *(Where?* I want to scream, *Where's the land? Has someone invented a Land-manufacturing machine?)*

The nasties say, *'Someone* has to pay the price for National Development'.

The point is that 56 million is more than a blip, folks. It's civil war.

Quite apart from the human cost of Big Dams, there are the staggering environmental costs. More than five million hectares of submerged forest, ravaged ecosystems, destroyed rivers, defunct, silted up reservoirs endangered wildlife, disappearing bio-diversity, and 10 million hectares of agricultural land that is now waterlogged and saline. Today there are more drought-prone and flood -prone areas in India than there where in 1947. Not a single river in the plains has potable water. Remember, 200 million Indians have no access to safe drinking water.

Planners, when confronted with past mistakes, say sagely, "Yes, it's true that mistakes have been made. But we're on a learning curve." The lives and livelihoods of 56 million people and all this environmental mayhem serves only to extend the majestic arc of their learning curve. When will they get off the curve and actually *learn*?

The evidence against Big Dams is mounting alarmingly. None of it appears on the balance sheet. There is no balance sheet. *There has not been an official audit, a comprehensive, post-project evaluation, of a single Indian Big Dam to see whether or not it has achieved what it set out to achieve.*

This is what is hardest to believe. That the Indian government's unshakable faith in Big Dams is based on *nothing*. No studies. No system of checks and balances. Nothing at all. And of course, those of us who question it are spies.

Is it unreasonable to call for a moratorium on the construction of Big Dams until "past mistakes" have been rectified and the millions of uprooted people have been truly recompensed and rehabilitated? It is the only way an industry that has so far been based on lies and false promises can redeem itself.

Now let me tell you about the Narmada Valley.

Of the series of 30 Big Dams proposed on the main river, four are mega-dams. Of these, only one—the Bargi Dam—has been completed. Three are under construction.

The Bargi Dam was completed in 1990. It cost 10 times more than was budgeted and submerged three times more land than engineers said it would. To save the cost and effort of doing a detailed survey, in order to mark the Full Reservoir Level, one monsoon the government closed the sluice gates and filled the reservoir without warning anybody. Water entered villagers' homes at night. They had to take their children, their cattle, their pots and pans and flee up the hillside. The Narmada Control Authority had estimated that 70,000 people from 101 villages would be displaced. Instead, when they filled the reservoir, 114,000 people from 162 villages were displaced. In addition, 26 government 'resettlement colonies' (which consisted of house plots but no agricultural land) were also submerged. Eventually there was no rehabilitation. Some 'oustees' got a meagre cash compensation. Most got nothing. Some died of starvation. Others moved to slums in Jabalpur where they work as rickshaw-pullers and construction labour.

Today, ten years after it was completed, the Bargi Dam irrigates only as much land as it submerged.

Only 5 per cent of the land its planners claimed it would irrigate. The government says it has no money to make the canals. Yet work has begun downstream on the mammoth Narmada Sagar Dam which will submerge 251 villages, on the Maheshwar Dam and of course, on the most controversial dam in history, the Sardar Sarovar.

The Sardar Sarovar Dam is currently 90 metres high. Its final projected height is 138 metres. It is located in Gujarat, but most of the villages that will be submerged by its gigantic reservoir are in Maharashtra and Madhyapradesh. The Sardar Sarovar Dam has become the showcase of India's Violation of Human Rights initiative. It has ripped away the genial mask of Dams-as-Development and revealed its brutish innards. I have written about it extensively in a previous essay (*The Greater Common Good, Outlook,* June 1999) so I'll be brief. The Sardar Sarovar Dam will displace close to half a million people. More than half of them do not officially qualify as "project-affected" and are not entitled to rehabilitation. It will submerge 13,000 hectares of deciduous forest.

In 1985, before a single study had been done, before anyone had any idea what the human cost or environmental impact of the dam would be, the World Bank sanctioned a $ 450-million loan for the dam. The ministry of environment's conditional clearance (without any studies being done) came in 1987! At no point in the decision-making process were the people to be affected consulted or even *informed* about the project. In 1993, after a spectacular struggle by the extraordinary Narmada Bachao Andolan (NBA), the people of the valley forced the Bank to withdraw from the project. The Gujarat government decided to go ahead with the project. In 1994, the NBA filed a petition in the Supreme Court. For six years, the court put a legal injunction on further construction of the dam. On October 18, 2000, in a shocking 2-1 majority judgement, the Supreme Court lifted the injunction. After having seen it fit to hold up the construction for six years, the court chastised (using unseemly, insulting language) the people of the Narmada Valley for approaching it too late and said that on these grounds alone their petition should be dismissed. It permitted construction to continue according to the guidelines laid down by the Narmada Water Disputes Tribunal.

It did this despite the fact that it was aware that the Tribunal Award has been consistently violated for 13 years. Despite the fact that none of the conditions of the environment ministry's clearance have been met. Despite the fact that 13 years have been passed and the government hasn't even produced a resettlement *plan*. Despite the fact that not a single village has been resettled according to the directives of the Tribunal. Despite the fact that the Madhya Pradesh (MP) Government has stated on oath that it has no land to resettle 'outsees' (80 per cent of them live in MP). Despite the fact that since construction began, the MP government has not given a single hectare of agricultural land to displaced families. Despite the fact that the court was fully aware that even families displaced by the dam at its current height have not been rehabilitated.

In other words, the Supreme Court has actually ordered and sanctioned the violation of the Narmada Water Disputes Tribunal Award.

"But this is the *problem* with the government", Mr and Mrs Well-Meaning say. "These things wouldn't happen with a private company. Things like resettlement and rehabilitation of poor people will be so much better managed."

The Maheshwar experience teaches you otherwise. In a private project, the only thing that's better managed is the corruption, the lies and the swiftness and brutality of repression. And, of course, the escalating costs.

In 1994, the project cost of the Maheshwar Dam was estimated at Rs 465 crore. In 1996, following the contract with the S.Kumars, it rose to Rs 1,569 crore. Today it stands at Rs 2,200 crore. Initially, 80 per cent of this money was to be raised from foreign investors. There has been a procession of them—Pacgen of the US, Bayernwerk, VEW, Siemens and the Hypovereinsbank of Germany. And now, the latest in the line of ardent suitors, Ogden of the US.

According to the NBA's calculations, the cost of the electricity at the factory gate will be Rs 6.55 per unit, which is 26 *times* more expensive than the existing hydel power in the state, five-and-a-half times more expensive than thermal power and four times more expensive than power from the central grid. (It's worth mentioning here that Madhya Pradesh today generates 1,500 MW more power than it can transmit and distribute.)

Though the installed capacity of the Maheshwar project is supposed to be 400 MW, studies using 28 years of actual river flow data show that 80 per cent of the electricity will be generated only during the monsoon months when the river is full. What this means is that most of the supply will be generated when it's least needed.

The S.Kumars have no worries on this count. They have Enron as a precedent. They have an escrow clause in their contract, which guarantees them first call on government funds. This means that however much (or however little) electricity they produce, whether anybody buys it or not, for the next 35 years they are guaranteed a minimum payment from the government of approximately Rs. 600 crore a year. This money will be paid to them even before the employees of the bankrupt SEB get their salaries. What did the S.Kumars do to deserve this largesse?

It isn't hard to guess.

So who's *actually* paying for this dam that nobody needs?

According to government surveys, the reservoir of the Maheshwar Dam will submerge 61 villages. Thirteen will be wholly submerged, the rest will lose their farmlands. As usual, none of the villagers were informed about the dam or their impending eviction. (Of course, if they go to court now they'll be told it's too late since construction has already begun.) The first surveys were done under a ruse that a railway line was being constructed. It was only in 1997, when blasting began at the dam site, that realisation dawned on the people and the NBA became active in Maheshwar. The agency in charge of the survey is the same one that was in charge of the surveys for the Bargi reservoir. We know what happened there.

People in the submergence zone of the Maheshwar dam say that the surveys are completely wrong. Some villages marked for submergence are at a higher level than villages that are not counted as project affected. Since the Maheshwar dam is located in the broad plains of Nimad, even a small miscalculation in the surveys will lead to huge discrepancies between what is marked for submergence and what is actually submerged. The consequences of these errors will be far worse than what happened at Bargi.

There are other egregious assumptions in the 'survey'. Annexure 6 of the resettlement plan states that there are 176 trees and 38 wells in all the affected 61 villages combined. The villagers point out that in just a single village—Pathrad—there are 40 wells and over 4,000 trees.

As with trees and wells, so with people. There is no accurate estimate of how many people will be affected by the dam. Even the project authorities admit that new surveys must be done. So far they've managed to survey only one out of the 61 villages. The number of affected households rose from 190 (in the preliminary survey) to 300 (in the new one.)

In circumstances like these, it's impossible for even the NBA to have an accurate idea of the numbers of project-affected people. Their rough guess is about 50,000. More than half of them are Kevats, Kahars and other Dalits... ancient communities of ferrymen, fisherfolk, sand quarriers and cultivators of the river-bed when the waters recede in the dry season. Most of them own no land, but the river sustains them and means more to them than anyone else. If the dam is built, thousands of them will lose there only source of livelihood. Yet simply because they are landless, they do not qualify as project-affected and will not be eligible for rehabilitation.

Jalud is the first of the 61 villages that is slated for submergence in the reservoir of the dam. As early as 1985, 12 families, mostly Dalit, who had small holdings near the dam site, had their land acquired. When they protested, cement was poured in to their water pipes, their standing crops were bulldozed, and the police occupied the land by force. All 12 families are now landless and work as wage labour. The new 'private' initiative has made no effort to help them.

According to the environmental clearance from the Central government, the people affected by the project ought to have been resettled three years ago, in 1997. To date, the S.Kumars haven't even managed to produce a list of project-affected people, let alone land on which they are to be resettled. Yet, construction continues. The S.Kumars are so well entrenched with the state government that they don't need to even *pretend* to cover their tracks.

This is how India Works.

This is the genesis of the Maheshwar Dam. This is the legacy that the Ogden Energy Group of the US is so keen to inherit. What they don't realise is that the fight is on. Over the last three years, the struggle against the Maheshwar Dam has grown into a veritable civil disobedience movement, though you wouldn't know it if you read the papers. The mainstream media is hugely dependent on revenue from advertising. The S.Kumars sponsor massive advertisements for their blended suitings. After their James Bond Campaign with Pierce Brosnan, they've signed India's biggest film star—Hrithik Roshan—as their star campaigner. It's extraordinary how much silent admiration and support a hunk in a blended suit can evoke.

Over the last two years, tens of thousands of villagers have captured the dam site several times and halted construction work. Protests in the region forced two companies, Bayernwerk and VEW of Germany, to withdraw from the project. The German company Siemens remained in the fray (angling for an export credit guarantee from Hermes, the German ECA). In the summer of 2000, the German Ministry of Economic Co-operation and Development sent in a team of experts headed by Richard Bissell (former chairman of the inspection panel of the World Bank) to do an independent review of the Resettlement and

Rehabilitation aspects of the project. The report published on the 15th of June this year, was unambiguous that resettlement and rehabilitation of people displaced by the Maheshwar Dam was simply not possible.

At the end of August, Siemens withdrew its application for a Hermes guarantee.

The people of the valley don't get much time to recover between bouts of fighting. In September, S.Kumars were part of the Indian Prime Minister's business entourage when he visited the US. Desperate to replace Siemens, they were hoping to convert their memorandum of understanding with Ogden into a final contract. That, fortunately (for Ogden as much as the people of Maheshwar), hasn't happened yet.

The only time I have ever felt anything close to what most people would describe as national pride was when I walked one night with 4,000 people towards the Maheshwar dam site, where we knew hundreds of armed policemen were waiting for us. From the previous evening, people from all over the valley had begun to gather in a village called Sulgaon. They came in tractors, in bullock carts and on foot. They came prepared to be beaten, humiliated and taken to prison.

We set out at three in the morning. We walked for three hours—farmers, fishermen, sandminers, writers, painters, film-makers, lawyers, journalists. All of India was represented. Urban, rural, touchable, untouchable. This alliance is what gives the movement its raw power, its intellectual rigour and its phenomenal tenacity. As we crossed fields and forded streams,I remember thinking—this is my land, this is the dream to which the whole of me belongs, this is worth more to me than anything else in the world. We were not just fighting against a dam. We were fighting for a philosophy. For a worldview.

We walked in utter silence. Not a throat was cleared. Not a bidi lit. We arrived at the dam site at dawn. Though the police were expecting us, they didn't know exactly where we would come from. We captured the dam site. People were beaten, humiliated and arrested.

I was arrested and pushed into a private car that belonged to the S.Kumars. I remember feeling a hot stab of shame—as quick and sharp as my earlier sense of pride. This was my land too. My feudal land. Where even the police is privatised. (On the way to the police station, they complained that the S.Kumars had given them nothing to eat all day.) That evening, there were so many arrests, the jail could not contain the people. The administration broke down and abandoned the jail. The people locked themselves in and demanded answers to their questions. So far, none have been forthcoming.

A Dutch documentary film-maker recently asked me a very simple question: What can India teach the world?

A documentary film-maker needs to *see* to understand. I thought of three places I could take him to.

First, to a 'Call Centre College' in Gurgaon on the outskirts of Delhi. I thought it would be interesting for a film-maker to see how easily an ancient civilisation can be made to abase itself completely. In a Call Centre College, hundreds of young English speaking Indians are being groomed to man the backroom operations of giant transnational companies. They are trained to answer telephone queries from the US and the UK (on subjects ranging from a credit card enquiry to advice about a malfunctioning washing machine.) On no account must the caller know that his or her enquiry is being attended to by an Indian, sitting at a desk on the outskirts of Delhi. The Call Centre Colleges train their students to speak in American and British accents. They have to read foreign papers so that they can chit chat about the news or the weather. On duty they have to change their given names. Sushma becomes Susie, Govind becomes Jerry, Advani becomes Andy. *(Hi! I'm Andy, gee, hot day innit? Shoot, how can I help ya?)*

They're paid exactly one-tenth of the salaries of their counterparts abroad. From all accounts, call centres are billed to become a trillion-dollar industry. Recently the Tatas announced their plans to re-deploy 20,000 of their retrenched workers in call centres after a brief 'period of training' for the business, such as, 'picking up the American accent slang'. The news report said that the older employees may find it difficult to work at night—a requirement for US-based companies, given the time difference between India and the US.

The second place I thought I'd take the film-maker to is an RSS shakha where the terrible back-lash to this enforced abasement is being nurtured and groomed. Where ordinary people march around in khaki shorts and learn that amassing nuclear weapons, religious bigotry, misogyny, homophobia, book burning and outright hatred are the ways in which to retrieve a nation's lost dignity. Here he might see for himself how the two arms of government work in synergy. How they have evolved and pretty near perfected an extraordinary pincer action—while one arm is busy selling the nation off in chunks, the other, to divert attention, is orchestrating a baying, howling, deranged chorus of cultural nationalism. It would be fascinating to actually see how the inexorable truthlessness of one process results in the naked, vulgar, terrorism perpetrated by the other. They're Siamese twins—Advani and Andy. They share organs. They have the ability to say two entirely contradictory things simultaneously, to hold all positions it all times. There's no separating them.

The third place I thought I 'd take him to is the Narmada Valley. To witness the ferocious, magical, magnificent, tenacious and above all non-violent resistance that has grown on the banks of that beautiful river.

What is happening to our world is almost too colossal for human comprehension to contain. But it is a terrible, terrible thing. To contemplate its girth and circumference, to attempt to define it, to try and fight it all at once, is impossible. The only way to combat it is by fighting specific wars in specific ways. A good place to begin would be the Narmada Valley. In the present circumstances, the only thing in the world worth globalising , is dissent.

Dissent with options. Dissent with imagination.

You'll find it in the Narmada Valley. The borders are open. Come on in. Let's bury Rumpelstiltskin.

Appendix : The Story of Rumpelstiltskin

One day a king was riding through a village in his kingdom when he heard a woman singing,

"My daughter has burnt five cakes today,

My daughter has burnt five cakes today."

It was the miller's wife who was cross with her daughter for being so careless. The king stopped as he wanted to hear her song again. The miller's wife hoped to impress the king so she sang,

"My daughter has spun fine gold today,

My daughter has spun fine gold today."

And she boasted that her daughter could spin straw into gold thread.

The king was greatly impressed.

"If your daughter will spin for me in my palace, I'll give her many presents. I might even make her my queen." he announced.

"What a wonderful chance," muttered the miller's wife under her breath. "We'll all be rich." Then out loud she said, "My daughter will be honoured, your Majesty."

The king took the girl back to the palace.

He ordered a spinning wheel to be placed in a room filled with straw.

"Spin this into gold by the morning or you will die," he commanded. Left alone, the poor girl wept bitterly. She could not spin straw into gold as her mother had boasted and she could not escape as the king had locked the door firmly behind him.

Suddenly a little man appeared from nowhere. He had a small pointed face and wore elfin clothes in green and brown.

"What will you give me, pretty girl, if I spin this straw into gold for you?" he asked.

"I will give you my necklace," the girl replied, "if you really can help me. Yet how can anyone do this task!"

At once the little man sat down by the spinning wheel. Singing strange songs, he spun all the straw into fine gold thread. Then taking the girl's necklace, with a skip and a hop and a stamp of his foot, he disappeared.

When the king unlocked the room the next morning he was astonished and delighted to see the skeins of golden thread. He sent delicious food to the miller's girl. But that evening he took her to another room with an even bigger pile of straw and a spinning wheel.

"Now spin this into gold," he ordered, "and I shall reward you well. But if you fail I shall chop off your head." He walked out, locking the miller's daughter in behind him.

The poor girl stared at the straw and the spinning

wheel. "What can I do now?" she cried, "I cannot turn straw into gold and the king will kill me if I fail."

Suddenly the same little man in elfin clothes stood before her.

"What will you give me this time if I spin your gold for you?"

"I'll give you my bracelet," said the miller's girl for she had nothing else to offer.

At once the little man set the spinning wheel whinring. Singing his weird songs, he quickly turned the straw into golden thread. Before down he had finished, and snatching the bracelet he was gone, with a skip and a hop and a stamp of his foot.

The king was delighted the next morning, and sent pretty clothes and good food up to the girl as a reward. "If this girl can really spin gold from straw," he thought greedily, "I shall always be rich if I make her my wife. But in case there is some trick I will try her once more."

So the third night the king took the miller's girl into another room with an even greater pile of straw and a spinning wheel.

"Spin this into gold," he commanded. "If you succeed, I shall marry you and you shall be queen. If you fail your head will be chopped off tomorrow."

Once more, as the girl wept bitterly before the pile of straw and the spinning wheel, the little man appeared from nowhere.

"I see you need my help again," he said. "How will you reward me this time if I save you life?"

"I have nothing to give," the miller's daughter said sadly. "Perhaps you should just go and leave me to my fate."

"Ah!" said the little man, "But if the straw is spun into gold tonight, you will become the queen. Will you promise to give me your first child when it is born?"

"Yes! Yes!" cried the girl. When this time came, she was sure she could save her child somehow.

So the little man sat and twirled the spinning wheel, beating his foot on the floor and singing his strange songs. Then with a skip and a hop and a stamp of his foot, once more he was gone.

The next day the king was delighted to see the gold spun from the huge pile of straw and he kept his promise. The miller's daughter became his wife and queen.

And as queen the miller's daughter forgot all about her promise to the little man. About a year later, a fine son was born, and she was horrified when one day the little man appeared.

"I have come to claim the child you promised me," he said, stamping his foot as he spoke.

The queen pleaded with him to release her from the promise.

"Take my jewels and all this gold," she begged, "only leave me my little son."

The little man saw her tears and said, "Very well.

You have three days in which to guess my name. You may have three gusses each night. If you fail on the third night, the baby is mine." Then he vanished.

The queen sent for all her servants and asked them to go throughout the kingdom asking if anyone had heard of the little man and if they knew his name. The first night the little man came she tried some unusual names:

"Is it Caspar?" she asked.

"No!" he said and stamped his foot in delight.

"It is Balschazzar?"

"No!" he said as he stamped his foot again.

"Is it Melchior?"

"No!" he cried. He stamped his foot and disappeared.

The next evening the queen thought she would try some everyday names. So when he appeared she asked,

"Is your name John?"

"No!" he said with his usual stamp.

"Is it Michael?"

"Is it James?"

"No! No!" he cried, stamping his foot each time. Then with a hop and a skip, triumphantly he disappeared.

The next day the queen was very sad for she could not see how she could guess the little man's name. She felt sure she would lose her baby that night.

The palace servants came back without any news except for one who returned to the palace towards the end of the day. He went straight to the queen and told her that at the very edge of the kingdom, under the mountains, he had seen a little man singing as he danced around a fire.

"What did he sing?" asked the queen breathlessly.

"Today I brew, tomorrow I bake,

Next day the queen's child I take

How glad I am that nobody knows

My name is Rumpelstiltskin."

The queen clapped her hands with joy and rewarded the servant. That night the little man appeared and asked if she had guessed his name.

"Is it Ichabod?"

"No!" he cried with pleasure as he stamped his foot.

"Is it Carl?"

"No!" he shouted as he laughed and stamped his foot.

"Is it..." the queen hesitated... "Is it Rumpelstiltskin?"

Now it was the queen's turn to laugh. The little man stamped his foot so hard it went through the floor. He disappeared in a flash and was never seen again.

Interview with Arundhati Roy
by N. Ram, Editor—Frontline
(January, 2001)

Arundhati Roy has rarely given extended interviews on her writing or the subjects she writes
about. She points out that what she wants to say is
contained in the writing. She made an exception
by giving the following extended interview, in her
New Delhi home, to Frontline's Editor, N.Ram.
In this, the writer speaks about the issues she es-
pouses, her response to her critics, and her views
on a writer's place in society. She also answers some
questions relating to *The God of Small Things*, re-
vealing why the novel has not been, and perhaps
will never be, made into a film.

N. Ram: Arundhati Roy, the Supreme Court judgment is unambiguous in its support for the Sardar Sarovar Dam. Is it all over? Are you, as the saying goes, running on empty?

Arundhati Roy: There are troubled times ahead, and yes, I think we—when I say 'we', I don't mean to speak on behalf of the NBA, I just generally mean people who share their point of view—yes, I think we *are* up against it. We do have our backs to the wall... but then, as another saying goes, 'It ain't over till the fat lady sings' [smiles]. Remember, there are a total of 30 Big Dams planned in the Narmada Valley. Upstream from the Sardar Sarovar, the people fighting the

Maheshwar dam are winning victory after victory. Protests in the Nimad region have forced several foreign investors—Bayernwerk, Pacgen, Siemens—to pull out. Recently, they managed to make Ogden Energy Group, an American company, withdraw from the project. There's a full-blown civil disobedience movement on there.

But yes, the Supreme Court judgment on the Sardar Sarovar is a tremendous blow—the aftershocks will be felt not just in the Narmada Valley, but all over the country. Wise men—L.C. Jain, Ramaswamy Iyer—have done brilliant analyses of the judgment. The worrying thing is not just that the Court has allowed construction of the dam to proceed, but the manner in which it disregarded the evidence placed before it. It ignored the fact that conditional environmental clearance for the project was given before a *single* comprehensive study of the project was done. It ignored the government of Madhya Pradesh's affidavit that it has no land to resettle the oustees, that in all these years M.P. has not produced a *single* hectare of agricultural land for its oustees. It ignored the fact that *not one* village has been resettled according to the directives of the Narmada Water Disputes Tribunal Award, the fact that 13 years after the project was given conditional clearance, *not a single* condition has been fulfilled, that there isn't even a rehabilitation Master

Plan—let alone proper rehabilitation. Most importantly, most urgently, it allowed construction to proceed to 90 metres despite the fact that the Court was fully aware that families displaced at the current height of the dam have not yet been rehabilitated—some of them haven't even had their land *acquired* yet! It has, in effect, *ordered* the violation of the Tribunal Award, It has indirectly endorsed the violation of human rights to life and livelihood. There will be mayhem in the Narmada Valley this monsoon if it rains—and of course, mayhem if it doesn't, because then there'll be dorught. Either way the people are trapped—between the Rain Gods and the Supreme Court Gods.

For the Supreme Court of India to sanction what amounts to submergence without rehabilitation is an extraordinary thing. Think of the implications—today, the India Country study done for the World Commission on Dams [WCD] says that Big Dams could have displaced up to *56 million people* in this country in the last 50 years! So far there has been, if nothing else at least a pretence, that rehabilitation has been carried out, even though we know that lakhs of people displaced half a century ago by the famous Bhakra Nangal Dam have *still* not been resettled. But now it looks as though we're going to drop even the charade of rehabilitation.

But the most worrying thing in the Sardar Sarovar judgment is the part where it says that once government begins work on a project, after it has incurred costs, the Court ought to have no further role to play. This, after the very same Court found enough cause in 1994 to hold up construction work for six whole years... With this single statement, the Supreme Court of India is abdicating its supreme responsibility. If the Court has no role to play in arbitrating between the state and its citizens in the matter of violations of human rights, then what is it here for? If justice isn't a court's business, then what *is*?

N. Ram: Why do you think things have come to this pass? This figure you have spoken of several times—between 33 million and 56 million people displaced by big dams in the last 50 years—it is hard to imagine something of this magnitude happening in another country without it being somehow taken into serious account...

Arundhati Roy: Without it being taken into account, without it giving pause for thought, without it affecting the nature of our country's decision-making process. The government doesn't even have a record of displaced people, they don't even count as statistics, it's chilling. Terrifying. After everything that has been written, said and done, the Indian government continues to turn a deaf ear to the protests. 695 big dams—40 per cent of all the big dams being built in the world—are being built in India as we speak. Yet India is the *only* country in the world that refused to allow the World Commission on Dams to hold a public hearing here. The Gujarat Government banned its entry into Gujarat and threatened its representatives with arrest! The World Commission on Dams was an independent commission set up to study the impact of large dams. There were twelve commissioners, some of them representatives of the international dam industry, some were middle-of-the-roaders and some were campaigners *against* dams. It was the first comprehensive study of its kind ever done. The report was released in London in November by Nelson Mandela. It's valuable because it's a negotiated document, nogotiated between two warring camps and signed by all the commissioners. I don't agree with everything that the WCD Report says, not by a long shot—but compared to the Supreme Court judgment that eulogises the virtues of big dams based on *no evidence what-soever,* the WCD Report is positively enlightened. It's as though the two were written in different centuries. One in the Dark Ages, one now. But it makes no difference here. There was a tiny ripple of interest in the news for a couple of days. Even that's died down. We're back to business as usual. As they say in the army—'Bash On Regardless'. Literally!

N. Ram: You must have an explanation, a

personal theory perhaps, of why the government is so implacable, so unwilling to listen?

Arundhati Roy: Part of the explanation—the relatively innocent part, I'd say—has to do with the fact that belief in Big Dams has become a reflex article of faith. Some people—particularly older planners and engineers—have internalised the Nehruvian thing about Big Dams being the Temples of Modern India. Dams have become India's secular gods—faith in them is impervious to argument. Another important part of the explanation has to do with the simple matter of corruption. Big Dams are gold mines for politicians, bureaucrats, the construction industry... But the really sad, ugly part has less to do with government than with the way our society is structured. More than 60 per cent of the millions of people displaced by dams are Dalit and Adivasi. But Adivasis account for only 8 per cent and Dalits about 15 per cent of our population. So you see what's happening here—a vast majority of displaced people don't even weigh in as real people.

And another thing—what percentage of the people who plan these mammoth projects are Dalit, Adivasi or even rural? Zero.

There is no egalitarian social contact *whatsoever* between the two worlds. Deep at the heart of the horror of what's going on, lies the caste system: this layered, horizontally divided society with no vertical bolts, no glue—no intermarriage, no social mingling, no human—*humane*—interaction that holds the layers together. So when the bottom half of society simply shears off and falls away, it happens silently. It doesn't create the torsion, the upheaval, the blowout, the sheer structural damage that it might, had there been the equivalent of vertical bolts. This works perfectly for the supporters of these projects.

But even those of us who do understand and sympathise with the issue, even if we feel concern, scholarly concern, writerly concern, journalistic concern—the press has done a reasonably persistent job of keeping it in the news—still, for the most part, there's no real *empathy* with those who pay the price. Empathy would lead to passion, to incandescent anger, to wild indignation, to action. Concern, on the other hand, leads to articles, books, Ph.Ds, fellowships. Of course, it is dispassionate enquiry that has created the pile-up of incriminating evidence against Big Dams. But now that the evidence *is* available and is in the public domain, it's time to do something about it.

Instead, what's happening now is that the relationship between concern and empathy is becoming oppositional, confrontational. When concern turns on empathy and says 'this town isn't big enough for the two of us,' then we're in trouble, big trouble. It means something ugly is afoot. It means concern has become a professional enterprise, a profitable business that's protecting its interests like any other. People have set up shop, they don't want the furniture disturbed. That's when this politics becomes murky, dangerous and manipulative. This is exactly what's happening now—any display of feeling, of sentiment, is being frowned upon by some worthy keepers of the flame. Every emotion must be stifled, must appear at the high table dressed for dinner. Nobody's allowed to violate the dress code or, god forbid, appear naked. The guests must not be embarrassed. The feast must go on...

But to come back to your question: as long as the protest remains civil and well-mannered, as long as we—the self-appointed opinion-makers—all continue to behave in respectable ways, as long as we continue to mindlessly defer to institutions that have themselves begun to cynically drop any pretence of being moral, just, or respectable—why should the governmnt listen? It's doing just fine.

N. Ram: Speaking of embarrassment, you have been criticised for embarrassing the NBA, for being tactless in your comments about the Supreme Court, for calling India a Banana Republic, for comparing the Supreme Court judgment to the NATO bombing of Yugoslavia...

Arundhati Roy: I'm being arraigned for bad

behaviour (laughs). I wear that criticism as a badge of honour. If 'tactless' was all I was about that judgment, then I'm guilty of an extreme form of moderation. As for embarrassing the NBA—the NBA has said and done far more radical things than I have... After the judgment, Baba Amte said—let me read this out—*"the judiciary at times wearing the cloak of priesthood, suffocates the human rights of the poor. Corruption and capital are given legitimacy instead of adhering to the rule of law..."* Its leader Medha Patkar was arrested for picketing the gates of the Supreme Court.

Anybody who thinks that *I* have been intemperate has their ear very far from the ground. They have no idea how people in the valley reacted to the judgment. Days after it came out, a spontaneous procession of youngsters buried it in a filthy public gutter in Badwani. I was there, I saw it happen—the rallying slogan was *'Supreme Court ne kya kiya? Nyaya ka satyanaash kiya'*—(What has the Supreme Court done? It has destroyed Justice!)

But I want to make it quite clear that I am an independent citizen. I don't have a Party line. I stated my opinion. Not carelessly, I might add, I said what I thought. If that embarrassed anybody, it's a pity, but it's too bad. But perhaps my critics should check back with the NBA before voicing their touching concern.

But in the time-honoured tradition of our worst

politicians, may I clarify what I *actually* said? I was talking to the press about the fact that the Supreme Court judgment had made things worse for the NBA than they were before it went to court. The Court ordered that the final arbiter of any dispute would be the Prime Minister. This is so clearly in contravention of the directives laid down by the Narmada Water Disputes Tribunal Award. I said that a country in which it is left to the Prime Minister to clear a large dam project without any scientific studies being done; in which it is left to the Prime Minister to decide the final height of a dam regardless of how much water there is in the river; in which it is left to the Prime Minister to decide whether or not there is land available for resettlement—sounds very much like a Banana Republic to me. What's the point of committees and Ministries and authorities if it's all up to Big Daddy in the end?

As for the business about the NATO bombing—I was talking to a not-very-bright journalist, it turns out. I said that when the developed countries were industrialising, most of them had colonies which they cannibalised on their way up. We, on the other hand, have no colonies, so we turn upon ourselves and begin to gnaw at the edges of our own societies. I told him that it reminded me of the tiger in the Belgrade zoo which, driven insane with fear by the NATO bombing, began to eat its own limbls. This was twisted into the absurd statement that was eventually published. But it's my fault. I should have known better than to try and explain this to a disinterested journalist.

N. Ram: What next? Where does the struggle go from here?

Arundhati Roy: I don't know, really. It has to move into a different gear. All our eyes are on the NBA, waiting for its next move. It will take some time to evolve a strategy. But they are extraordinary people—brilliant. I have never met a group of people with their range of skills—their mobilisation abilities, their intellectual rigour, their political acumen. Their ability to move effortlessly from a dharna in Jalsindhi to arguing a subtle legal point in the Supreme Court, to making a presentation about the situation in the valley which leaves the World Bank no option but to pull out. The monsoon will be a terrible time for them—if it rains, people will need help on an emergency footing. The whole Adivasi belt will go under.

You see, while the rest of us sit around arguing about how much we ought to respect the Supreme Court judgment, the people in the valley have no option. They can hardly be expected to respectfully accept their own disposition. They will fight—How? is the question, and a very important one. The judgment, apart from what it says about the Sardar Sarovar, has

sent out another very grave signal. After all, the 15-year
-old struggle in the valley has so far been a spectacularly
non-violent one. Now if that has come to naught,
yielding nothing, I fear to think about what must be
going through people's heads. They watch as the world
around them gets more and more violent—as
kidnappings, hijackings and the events that unfold in
another valley further north grab the attention of the
government and yield instant results. Already extremist
groups have taken up position in parts of Madhya
Pradesh. I'm sure they're watching the Narmada Valley
with great interest. I don't know what would happen if
the NBA were to lose ground. I worry. I really do...

It's something the govenment must think very
seriously about. A 15-year-old non-violent poeple's
movement is an extraordinary, magnificent thing. If it
is dismissed in this contemptuous fashion, if violence
is the only thing that forces the government to the
negotiating table, then anarchy lurks around the
corner.

Meanwhile in Gujarat, interesting, predictable
things are happening. The false propaganda, the
deliberate misinformation about the Sardar Sarovar is
all coming home to roost. As long as the project was
stalled, as long as it was a *potential* dam, it was easy to sell
to voters as a miracle dam—the Sardar Sarovar will
mend your bad knee, will produce your daughter's

dowry, will serve you breakfast in bed. But major disputes over the water have already begun. People in Kutch and Saurashtra are waking up to the Big Con. The Kutch and Saurashtra branch of the BJP boycotted the inauguration of construction ceremony at the dam site. You know what happened there—three BJP Ministers had their official Cielos burnt by an irate BJP mob, one Minister was hurt and had to be airlifted out. The Kutch Jal Sankat Nivaran Samiti has a case against the government in court asking for construction to be stayed until Kutch is given its fair share of water. But a most interesting development is that the spokesperson of the Sardar Sarovar dam, the public face of the pro-dam lobby—Narmada Minister Jai Narain Vyas—was unceremoniously sacked recently. In the long run, it's probably good for Vyas—he'll be associated with the 'victory', but not with the murky politics of who gets the water. You can see it happening before your eyes: consensus in Gujarat is quickly coming unstuck.

Still, the honest answer to your question is: I don't really know what next. The answer will come, should come, from the people of the Narmada Valley.

N. Ram: Have you read Ramachandra Guha's tirade against you in *The Hindu?*

Arundhati Roy: (Smiles) Tirades. Plural. Yes, yes, of course I have. He's become like a stalker who shows up at my doorstep every other Sunday. Some days he comes alone. Some days he brings his friends and family, they all chant and stamp... It's an angry little cottage industry that seems to have sprung up around me. Like a bunch of keening god-squadders, they link hands to keep their courage up and egg each other on—Aunt Slushy the novelist who's hated me for years, Uncle Defence Ministry who loves big dams, Little Miss Muffet who thinks I should watch my mouth. Actually, I've grown quite fond of them and I'll miss them when they're gone. It's funny, when I wrote *The God of Small Things,* I was attacked by the Left—when I wrote *The End of Imagination,* by the Right. Now I'm accused by Guha and his Ra-Ra club of being—simultaneously— extreme left, extreme right, extreme green, RSS, Swadeshi Jagran Manch *and* by some devilish sleight of hand, on Guha's side too! Goodness, he's skidding on his own tail!

I don't know what it is with me and these academics-cum-cricket statisticians—Guha's the third one that I seem to have sent into an incensed orbit. Could it be my bad bowling action?... (laughs)

N. Ram: Why have you chosen not to respond to Guha? Do you, as many others seem to, dismiss it as just a bad case of envy?

Arundhati Roy: No, no, not at all. That would be too convenient, too easy. One could end up saying that about everybody who was critical. No, I think that would be unfair. I'd say it's far more complex and interesting than that. Guha's outburst is dressed up as an attack on my 'style'—but it's not really that at all. If you part the invective, you'll see that our differences are serious, and seriously political. Chittaroopa Palit of the NBA has done a wonderful dissection of Guha's politics in her article "The historian as gate-keeper" (*Frontline,* January 5, 2001).

My style, my language, is not something superficial, like a coat that I wear when I go out. My style is *me* - even when I'm at home. It's the *way* I think. My style *is* my politics. Guha claims that we - he and I - are 'objectively' on the same side. I completely disagree. We are worlds apart, our politics, our arguments. I'm inclined to put as great a distance as possible between the Guhas of the world and myself.

Take his book - his biography of Verrier Elwin. It's competent and cleanly written. But our political differences *begin* with his choice of subject—personally, I think we've had enough, come on, *enough* stories about white men, however interesting they are, and their adventures in the heart of darkness. As a subject for a biography, frankly, I'm much more interested in Kosi Elwin, his Gond wife.

And the title of his book! - *Savaging the Civilized. Verrier Elwin, His Tribals, and India. His* tribals! *His* tribals? For heaven's sake! Did he own them? Did he buy them? There's a bog, a marsh, a whole political swampland stretching between us right here. But it's his other work, his history books—he calls himself an ecological historian, you know that, don't you?

N. Ram: Yes, I believe so...

Arundhati Roy: Well, he's co-authored two books. One claims to be *An Ecological History of India,* nothing less, the other he calls *Ecology and Equity.* The sub-title is *The Use and Abuse of Nature in Contemporary* India and it was published as recently as 1995. In his ecological history, big dams don't merit *so much as a mention.* The other one has a thumbnail sketch of the struggle against big dams, and a cursory, superficial account of the struggle in the Narmada Valley. For someone who sets himself up as a chronicler of the ecological history of a country that is the third largest builder of big dams in the world, that has 3,600 big dams which have displaced may be up to 56 million people, that have submerged *millions* of acres of prime forest land, that have led to the waterlogging and salinisation of vast areas, that have destroyed estuarine ecosystems and drastically altered the ecology of almost every river in this country - wouldn't you say that the man has missed a wee thing or two! For goodness' sake — today, big dams are *the* staging ground for the most contentious debates on ecology, equity, social justice, bureaucratic and political intrigue, international finance and corruption on an unimaginable sacle. Why does *none* of this merit attention from this ecological historian?

I'll tell you why: no amount of research, however painstaking, can make up for political vacuousness. If you don't ask the right questions, you don't get the right answers. If your politics is clear, if you had your ear to the ground, you woudn't, you couldn't *possibly,* miss your mark so completely.

Look at the work of people like Ashish Kothari, Ramesh Billorey, Claude Alvarez, Himanshu Thakker, Shripad Dharmadhikary, and further afield, Edward Goldsmith, Nicholas Hildeyard, Patrick McCully—McCully's book, *Silenced Rivers,* is a dazzling analysis of the ecology and politics of big dams. Even someone like Anil Agarwal, though his views on the subject differ from those of the NBA—at least he engages with the issue. Their work is out there, it's vital stuff, it occupies centre-stage in the debate - but let's face it, all of this puts Mr. Guha in an extremely embarrassing position. He's like one of the creatures that didn't make it onto the ark. An ecological historian who missed the boat completely.

Sublimating shame into anger, we all know, is a common human failing. So what does Guha do? He picks the most visible target from amongst those who he feels are embarrassing him, and lets fly. If he had disputed my facts, if he had taken apart my argument,

I could have respected him. I look forward to that devastating, incisive, logical tearing apart of my argument...Actually, that's a complete lie, I'm quite grateful that Guha's made such a spectacle of himself. Does he have *anything* substantial to say? Apart from insulting me personally, deliberately, wilfully, maliciously, Guha has no argument against my argument, nothing to say about my facts. So he tries to legislate on how I ought to *feel* about them. Never was there a more passionate indictment of passion, a more hysterical denunciation of hysteria - he's right, I *am* hysterical. I'm screaming from the bloody rooftops. And he and his smug little club are going *Shhhh...you'll wake the neighbours!* But I want to wake the neighbours, that's my whole point. I *want* everybody to open their eyes.

Anyway, as far as I am concerned, it's not his insults I find as corny as the rest of it - his pronouncements about what's good for the environmental movement and what's not - the quintessence of which is, that *he's* good for the movement and I'm not. His pronouncements on what constitutes good writing, His does, mine dosen't. His unsolicited advice - advice to the NBA to disengage from me, advice to me to stop writing political essays and go back to literature. I mean apart from being someone with the Jurassic notion that politics and literature are mutually exclusive, who *is* he - the headboy? Cupboard captain? What's next? Is he going to put me on a diet? Choose my wardrobe? Sentence me to mustard bellbottoms for a whole month?

N. Ram: Why have you not responded to Guha's charges?

Arundhati Roy: Well, for one because I thought that four Sundays in a row (he's already used up three) discussing Arundhati Roy's work would be a bit much for readers...and anyway, how does one respond to a Punch and Judy show?

Guha hasn't really read my work —he's ransacked it, wearing lenses so thick with animus that they blur his vision. He's virtually imagined the essays he wishes I'd written in order for him to demolish with his piercing wit and intellect, while his friends and colleagues nod and grin. Any response from me would end up sounding like—oh, I didn't say this, I did'nt mean that... But if he can't be bothered to read my work carefully, why bother with a response?

Let me give you an example of what I mean: Guha tries to ridicule me for comparing big dams to nuclear bombs. But I've *never* done that - my essay says... here's exactly what it says - [reads]:

"Big Dams are to a nation's 'development' what nuclear bombs are to its military arsenal. They are both weapons of mass destruction, both weapons governments use to control their own people, both twentieth century emblems that mark a point in time when human intelligence has outstripped its own instinct for survival..."

Surely Guha ought to know that this, in the English language, is what's called a relative analogy. In a relative analogy, one is comparing two relationships. I'm saying that big dams and nuclear bombs are both political instruments extremely undemocratic political instruments. But I'm not saying bombs are dams. I'm not saying that dams are radioactive when they explode or that nuclear bombs irrigate agricultural land. If I say Amitabh Bachchan is to film stars what Coke is to fizzy drinks, I'm not comparing Amitabh Bachchan to a Coke or saying that film stars are fizzy drinks. In algebra, if say x:y what w:r, it doesn't mean I'm saying x = w.

This is just one small example, there are other more sinister ones. For instance, he picks out one sentence from my new essay *Power Politics* that was published recently in *Outlook*. It says:

"When the history of India's miraculous leap to the forefront of the Information Revolution is written, let it be said that 56 million Indians (and their children and their children's children) paid for it with everything they ever had."

Here's how Guha scores one of the more tragic

'own goals' since Escobar - you know what happened to Escobar! Guha isolates the sentence out of context and kicks it towards his own goal, then flies to the goal post to stage a spectacular save. He has to use his instinct to decide whether to dive to his left or right. He dives - surprise surprise - to his extreme right. It's not the horror of 56 million displaced people that bothers him. It's my reference to the Information Revolution, which was used to compare the meteoric development of one sector of the Indian economy with the horrific dispossession of another. Guha gratuitously makes out that I'm attacking - not just attacking - being "grossly slanderous" to the IT gaints, Tata, Wipro and I forget who else—he actually names particular companies... *I don't!* Having invented the insult, our intrepid knight in shining armour rallies to their defence. Is he real? Is he looking for friends in high places? Or has he just stunned himself on the goalpost?

N. Ram: Talking about your essay The Greater Common Good, critics like Guha and B.G. Verghese say that it's sentimental without being factual, that it romanticises Adivasi life-styles...

Arundhati Roy: That's pretty rich coming from the ecologist who missed the ark! I don't want to sound arrogant—this is the trouble about defending oneself, immodesty goes with the territory! Sentimental without being factual? Look, just because I don't wave my footnotes in people's faces and don't do the academic heavy breathing stuff, it doesn't mean I haven't studied the subject in depth. I don't believe that there's a single fact or argument—social, ecological, economic or political—about the Sardar Sarovar dam that's missing, or that has not been addressed, in my essay. For this I have to thank the NBA for making available to me every document at its disposal—and all the people who've published wonderful work on this issue over the years. I'm talking of Himanshu Thakker, L.C. Jain, the FMG Report, Ramaswamy Iyer, Shripad Dharmadhikary, the Morse Committee Report, Rahul Ram's booklet *Muddy Waters*, Ashish Kothari... I owe a lot to long, sparky conversations with brilliant people in the valley, to *Kaise jeebo re*—Jharana Jhaveri and Anurag Singh's documentary film, which first sent me on my travels in the Narmada Valley... It's a long, long list and it's been more vital and insightful and instructive than doing years of research in a library.

As for the charge of romanticising Adivasi lifestyles—I thought the time when that sort of thing sent a frisson of excitement through the academic community had come and gone. I mean, come on—even the good old Gujarat Government feeds at that foetid trough. When I was writing *The Greater Common Good* I was acutely aware of two things: One, that I was not going to write on 'behalf' of anyone but myself because I think that's the most honest thing to do—in our society particularly, the politics of 'representation' is complicated and fraught with danger and dishonesty. Two, I was not writing an anthropological account of the lifestyles of people that I knew very little about. I was writing about social justice, about the politics of involuntary displacement, about what happens to people who are forcibly uprooted from an environment they know well and dumped in a world they know nothing about—a world in which, instead of a forest and a river and farmlands, they have unemployment and a tin shack. It's an unfair, unequal bargain for anybody—Adivasi or Aggarwal. At no point in my essay have I even attempted to describe Adivasi lifestyle, let alone romanticise it. Here's an early passage from *The Greater Common Good* (reads):

"...Let me say at the outset that I'm not a city-basher. I've done my time in a village. I've had first-hand experience of the isolation, the inequity and the potential savagery of it. I'm not an anti-development junkie or a proselytiser for the eternal upholding of custom and tradition..."

Does that sound particularly romantic? The fact is I grew up in a village—not an Adivasi village, but a village neertheless. As a child, all I ever dreamed of was escaping. I don't need to do 'research' or 'field-work' or write a Ph.D. to figure out what goes on. Anyone who's read The *God of Small Things* could work that out. If I do romanticise anything it's the freedom, the anonymity of urban life...

N. Ram: I'm sorry to go on about this, but Guha also denounces your work as self-indulgent and unoriginal. A serious charge against a fiction writer, wouldn't you say?

Arundhati Roy: Self-indulgence is not the kind of charge that one can refute. If I *am* self-indulgent then... what can I say? I'll stand in the corner and hang my head in shame! (laughs) But I think that the accusation has really to do with the fact that I often write in the first person. Like I said, I do that deliberately. I guess academics and journalists are trained to believe that saying "I" is somehow anathema—because they're supposed to come across as objective. Of course that's nonsense—a person who conceals his or her identity is no more objective than a person who reveals it. *Any* clued-in anthropologist should know that. For an artist, a painter, a writer, a singer, introspection—contemplating the self, placing yourself in the picture to see where you fit—is often what art is all about. For a writer, to use the first person is a common narrative device. It's not just crudity, it's a *fallacy*, to equate this with self-indulgence. Mind you, this is not the only time that Guha shows a reflexive hostility towards writers and an opacity to literature.

There's a fine but important difference between self-indulgence and self-awareness. Self-awareness, in this case, is being aware—when you write—that you are complicit, that you are a beneficiary of the terrible politics of the society in which you live. When you reveal who you are and how you have benefited. Self-indulgence is when, masquerading as a concerned academic, you fill the Sunday papers with personal invective against somebody you don't like, and follow that up by selectively publishing your friends' personal letters of support, and then your rejoinder that supports their support... and so on.

As for the charge of being unoriginal—when one is writing to advocate a political position, or in support of a people's movement that has been yelling its lungs out for the last fifteen years, one is not *trying* to be original, one is adding one's voice to theirs in order for *them* to be heard. Almost by definition, one is reiterating what they are saying. My essays are not about me or my brilliance or my originality or lack of it. They're not meant to be a career move—they're about re-stating the issue, they're about saying the *same* things over and over again...

N. Ram: You actually do say something about this in your essays...

Arundhati Roy: Yes, I'm flattered that you remember. Here, from *The End of Imagination [Frontline*, August 14, 1998) [reads]:

"There can be nothing more humiliating for a writer of fiction to have to do than to re-state a case that has, over the years, already been made by other people... and made passionately, eloquently and knowledgeably. But I am prepared to grovel. To humiliate myself abjectly, because in the circumstances, silence would be indefensible..."

And again, in *The Cost of Living* [*Frontline*, February 18, 2000], my Nehru Lecture on Big Dams:

"If you're a writer, you tend to keep those aching eyes open... Every day you are reminded that there is no such thing as innocence. And every day you have to think of new ways of saying old and obvious things. Things about love and greed. Things about politics and governance. About power and powerlessness... things that must be said over and over again..."

You see, once again Guha is guilty of flabby conclusions drawn from sloppy reading. Frankly, between his suspect politics and slapdash scholarship, a woman's spoiled for choice. Does anyone have the right to defame someone in such careless, wanton fashion? I think he owes me a public apology.

N. Ram: What about the charge that you simplify things, express them in black and white?

Arundhati Roy: I don't *simplify* things. I try and

explain complicated things *in simple language*. That's an entirely different enterprise. I find it offensive, this notion that things are too complicated to explain to an ordinary reader—again, this coterie, this club-mentality. I write about things that vitally affect people's lives. To say that things are too complicated to explain is just not good enough. They *must* be explained. Experts love to hijack various aspects of an issue—displacement, rehabilitation, drainage, hydrology—and carry them off to their lairs where they guard them against the curiosity of the interested layperson. But eventually it's not rocket science. It's about our daily lives. All these things must be understood, connected up and explained—simply and cogently. It's not enough to accuse me of simplifying things—how? what? where? Be specific. I can handle it. Everybody needs to know and understand what's going on. Not just the headboy and cupboard captain or the people who went to good schools. Not explaining something is a way of wresting power and holding onto it. It's a way of making yourself seem important, of trying to sound cleverer than you are. Of course I understand, there's jobs and money in that. But beyond a point, it becomes vulgar...

As for my monochromatic vision, things *are* more black and white than we like to admit. The subtlety is seeping out of our lives at a pretty nifty pace.

N. Ram: One of the more persistent criticisms of

the NBA and you is that you are Negativists, Nay sayers...

Arundhati Roy: Ah yes, that's the "Has Medha Patkar ever made a gobar gas plant?" school of thought. I just don't understand it. Big Dams wreak havoc. They have displaced millions of people, destroyed rivers and estuaries, submerged forests. The Narmada Valley project alone will submerge 4,000 square kilometres of forest. How does the fight to save this count as negativity? If there's a forest fire raging and someone's trying to put it out, is it negativism or is it conservation? If everything is destroyed there'll be nothing left to conserve! The NBA has been an inspiration to people's movements all over the world—how can you knock this? Any *one* of its activists is worth more national pride than all the Miss Worlds and Miss Universes put together a thousand times over. There are amazing people doing the most wonderful work in water-harvesting and water management all over India. Premjibhai Patel of Upleta, Manubhai Mehta of Savarkundla, the Tarun Bharat Sangh in Alwar and hundreds of others dotted across the country. But the fire-fighters and the water-harvesters are *both* part of the alternative solution. *Neither* would be much good without the other. One makes space for the other. The NBA is like an ice-breaker—a ship that clears the way through cliffs of ice for other ships to sail through. There's no need for

Medha Patkar to prove herself by designing a gobar gas plant, or for Rejinder Singh of the Tarun Bharat Sangh to prove himself by leading a dharna. They *both* do what they do wonderfully well. Pitting them against each other is small-minded, and it's destructive.

And while criticising the NBA, what does Mr. Guha hold up as his alternative vision? Dr. Pushpangandan, who collects rare medicinal plants—there won't be many of those around if the forests disappear. And JFM (Joint Forest Management) schemes in Bengal. I mean: what's he trying to say? That the World Bank and the Ford Foundation are the new radicals in town? The new people's movements? What's this? A wonky worldview? Or a grateful nudge and a wink to old friends?

N. Ram: In his attack on your new essay *Power Politics* published in *Outlook* [November 27, 2000], Guha says—and I quote: "...instead of turning on globalisation... we should come to terms with it, bend it as best we can to our interests—if we want to hold our own against foreign capital, we must encourage innovation by our technologists and entrepreneurs, not mock them as Roy does." Your comment?

Arundhati Roy: I'm getting a bit tired of this bloke. You know, I think he must have read someone else's essay. Because I haven't yet—at least not that I'm aware of—written an essay on globalisation. *Power*

Politics, for anyone who's prepared to read it and not just the blurb on the cover of *Outlook,* is an essay that argues specifically against the privatisation and corporatisation of *essential infrastructure.* The word 'globalisation' is not mentioned in the entire essay, not *once.* However, if and when I do write about globalisation, I can assure you that my views on the subject will be very different from Guha's.

But to answer his charge that I have mocked our technologists—take a look at this, it's a passage from *Power Politics:*

"The First World needs to sell, the Third World needs to buy—it ought to be a reasonable business proposition. But it isn't. For many years, India has been more or less self-sufficient in power equipment. The Indian public sector company, Bharat Heavy Electricals Ltd. (BHEL), manufactured and even exported world-class power equipment. All that's changed now. Over the years, our own government has starved it of orders, cut off funds for research and development and more or less edged it out of a dignified existence. Today BHEL is no more than a sweet shop. It is being forced into 'joint ventures' (one with GE, one with Siemens) where its only role is to provide cheap labour while they provide the equipment and the technology. Why? Why does more expensive, imported foreign equipment suit our bureaucrats and politicians better? We all know why. Because graft is factored into the deal. Buying equipment from your local store is just not the same thing."

Does this sound like I'm *mocking* our technologists? Seriously, are we talking about the *same* essay? Is there some other Arundhati Roy? Arundhati Rao? Aradhana Roy? Does she write essays for *Outlook* and *Frontline*? And this man lectures me about intellectual probity?

The globalisation debate has a very interesting spin on it—all its admirers, from Bill Clinton, Kofi Annan, A.B. Vajpayee to the cheering brokers in the stalls, all of them say the same lofty things: if we have the right institutions of governance in place—effective courts, good laws, honest politicians, participative democracy, a transparent administration that respects human rights and gives people a say in decisions that affect their lives—*then* the globalisation project will work for the poor as well.

My point is that if all this was in place, then almost *anything* would succeed: socialism, communism, you name it. Everything works in Paradise, even a poor old Banana Republic! But in an imperfect world, is it globalisation that's going to bring us all this bounty? Is that what's happening here now that India is on the fast tract to the free market? Does any *one* thing on that lofty list apply to the Narmada issue? Has the Supreme Court been just and accountable? State institutions transparent? Have people had a say, have they even been *informed* of decisions that vitally affect their lives? The answer is no, no, no... And strange to say—in this beleaguered democracy, is it the votaries of globalisation who are out there on the streets demanding accountability and responsible government? Of course not! And when someone else does—the NBA, or another people's movement, or an unfortunate private citizen, and has to contend with the police or, worse, academics with dubious politics— do these guys spring to their defence?

N. Ram: People have said that your essay *Power Politics* is self-contradictory because it is an argument against the market and globalisation by one who is placed at the heart of the global market for celebrity-hood.

Arundhati Roy: People have said? [chuckles] It's the old boy again, isn't it—what's his thesis this time? That *all* celebrities *must* support globalisation? Or that all writers who sell more than a certain number of copies of a book must support globalisation? What's the cut-off? Thirty thousand copies? Do language editions count? Audio books? Braille?

N. Ram: I learned that *The God of Small Things* has sold six million copies in some forty languages. Your agent, David Godwin, also tells me that you've turned down offers for film rights from all over the world, including Hollywood. Are you waiting for the right director? Can we ever expect to see a film version of your novel?

Arundhati Roy: No... it's not about the right director. I don't think my book would make a good film. Besides, I don't think cinema *has* to be the last stop for literature, for novels. I had written two feature screen-plays before I started writing *The God of Small Things*. I was feeling a little confined by the 'externality' of cinema. I wanted to be free to write from *within*, from *inside* people's hearts and heads. I wanted to feel free to write a whole page describing the moon and the trees in the river, not just have to write *Scene 21. Ext. Night. River.*

Perhaps *because* I was a sreenwriter, I set out to write a stubbornly visual but unfilmable book, And I did. The most visual thing about *The God of Small Things* are the *feelings.* How would you film lonely, frightened little Rahel communing with a kangaroo-shaped waste bin in Cochin Airport? I don't see cinema capturing the magic whisper, the helicopter kisses, the secret breathing of a cement kangaroo. Not unless you were making the Walt Disney version.

Also, I think that each reader of *The God of Small Things* has his or her own version of the film running inside their heads—there are six million different versions of the film. It would be a pity, don't you think, to let a single film-maker extinguish and appropriate all those versions, and force-fit them into a single, definitive one. This decentralised democracy is fine by me (smiles).

And this may sound silly, but I couldn't bear the idea of seeing actors play Estha, Rahel, Velutha, Ammu, Chacko... it would kill me. I love them too much. I always will.

N. Ram: It's interesting that Prime Minister Vajpayee has been vacationing in a resort in Kerala made internationally famous by *The God of Small Things*. The media have been full of this connection...

Arundhati Roy: (smiles)...yes. *"The History House. Whose doors were locked and windows open. With cool stone floors and dim walls and billowing ship-shaped shadows on the walls. Where plump, translucent lizards lived behind old pictures and waxy, crumbling ancestors with tough toe-nails and breath that smelled of yellow maps gossiped in sibilant, papery whispers..."* I know that bit by heart. When I was a child it was on old, abandoned, crumbling house that filled my imagination. It's odd, when the Prime Minister goes vacationing in the setting of your worst, most private, childhood terrors. But wasn't it Toni Morrison who said something like "literature is a very private thing, fashioned for public comsumption?" It's funny how my terrors have become a tourist paradise... but it's okay. I'm a big girl now (laughs).

N. Ram: Coming back to the issue of celebrity-hood—what's your relationship with it? How does it affect your writing? How do you deal with it?

Arundhati Roy: Celebrity-hood—I hate that word. How do I deal with it? When Rock Hudson's career was on the skids, if he heard of a friend or colleague who was doing well, he'd say "Damn him, I hope he dies." That's a bit how I feel about my celebrity-hood. When I see a picture of myself in the papers, I feel hostile towards my public self and say "Damn her, I hope she dies"... (smiles).

But actually, it's a very, very difficult thing for a person to come to terms with. For a while I thought it would drive me clean crazy. But I think I'm beginning to get the hang of it now. I worked it out from first principles—I'm a writer *first* and a celebrity next. I'm a writer who *happens* to have become, for the moment, a celebrity. As a matter of principle, I never do anything because I'm a celebrity. I don't inaugurate things, I don't appear as a chief guest anywhere, I don't 'grace' occasions, I don't do chat shows, I don't do interviews—

unless of course I'm rubbishing ecological historians!—or have something very specific to say.

But I also don't *not* do the things I *want* to do. I live, I love, I bum around, but above all, I write. And I support what I write. The celebrity part just trails along behind me making a heck of a noise—like a tin can attached to a cat's tail. I can't take it off—but it'll fall off on its own sooner or later. For now, I try to ignore it. Of course, it's not that simple. Every time I show up at an NBA dharna—and whether or not I show up is always a collective decision taken *with* them—the Press invariably reports that I 'led' it along with Medha. Now that's ridiculous! Ridiculous to equate us in any way, ridiculous to imply that I *lead* anything, leave alone the NBA. Fortunately, both Medha and I are aware of the double-edged nature of media attention. As I keep saying, she's the good one, I'm the bad one, and the bad news is that we're friends!

N. Ram: How does all this affect your writing? It's given you a lot of space to say what you want to say. Does that put any pressure on you? Do you run the risk of becoming a rag-bag of good causes?

Arundhati Roy: Make no mistake, it's not the tin can, not celebrity-hood, that's given me the space. It's my writing. I'm very clear on that one. I'm a celebrity *because* I'm a writer, not the other way around. After all, you or Vinod Mehta of *Outlook*—you're not running a soup kitchen, are you? You give me the space because it's worth it to you, because you know that I am read.

But if you're asking whether the fact that I *know* the space is available puts pressure on me—it does. At times. Because for me, to say *nothing* is as political an act as to say what I *do* say. There are these two voices virtually at war within me—one that wants me to dive underground and work on another book, another that refuses to let me look away, that drags me deep into the heart of what's going on around me. As for becoming a ragbag of good causes—you're right, the pressure is tremendous. Simply because horror lurks around every corner, and it's hard to listen to an account of it and then say that you can do nothing to help. But, you know, for me to become an ambassador of good causes would do injustice to the causes and a great violene to my writing self—and that's something that I will not sacrifice. At any cost. A singer sings, a painter paints, a writer writes. For some it's a profession. For others it's a calling. One does it because one must.

N. Ram: It sounds like a lonely place that you work from. What do you find most difficult about being who you are and doing what you do?

Arundhati Roy: Well, every writer—good, bad, successful or not—who's sitting at a desk looking at a blank piece of paper, is lonely. It's probably the loneliest work in the world. But once the work is done, it's different. I'm not lonely at all—I'm the opposite of lonely. How can I, of all people, complain? I like to think that if by chance I were to become completely destitute, I could spend the rest of my life walking into people's homes and saying, "I wrote *The God of Small Things*, will you give me lunch?" It's a wonderful feeling. When I go to the Narmada Valley, I see my essay being read in Hindi, in Gujarati, in Marathi—even translated orally into Bhilali. I see parts of it being performed as a play. What more could a writer ask for? How much less lonely can I be?

It's true that I write about contentious things. Closer to home, there's some hostility. Each time I step out I hear the snicker-snack of knives being sharpened, I catch the glint of scimitars in the sun. But that's good. It keeps me sharp—fit, alert, it focusses my thought, hones my argument, makes me very careful about what I say and how I say it. On the whole, it isn't a bad university to go to. I don't have the luxury of carelessness that some of my critics do.

N. Ram: Well, even Ramachandra Guha applauds you for your courage and the NBA for its loyalty to you.

Arundhati Roy: Courage and loyalty? They sound like kind words for a good horse. D'you think that's what he meant when he called us 'neigh-sayers'? (laughs helplessly)... Sorry about that, Ram!

IBD / 5/01